FOR THOSE WHO MOURN

A CROWN OF BEAUTY INSTEAD OF ASHES

LYNDA MUSILWA

WESTBOW
PRESS®
A DIVISION OF THOMAS NELSON
& ZONDERVAN

WestBow Press books may be ordered through booksellers or by contacting:

WestBow Press
A Division of Thomas Nelson & Zondervan
1663 Liberty Drive
Bloomington, IN 47403
www.westbowpress.com
1 (866) 928-1240

ISBN: 978-1-4908-3461-0 (sc)
ISBN: 978-1-4908-3462-7 (e)

Library of Congress Control Number: 2014907161

Printed in the United States of America.

WestBow Press rev. date: 8/28/2015

Contents

Foreword vii

I. Introduction 1

II. "He shall be called Emmanuel" - Isaiah 7:14 7

III. Angel Girl 9

IV. His voice in the storm 11

    God is faithful. 11

    Take time to grieve 13

    There is a wound only God can heal. 15

    The Holy Spirit is gentle. 17

    Pain is part of life on earth. 18

    God is with us. 19

    Jesus conquered the grave! 21

    One day at a time 22

    A broken heart can sing. 23

    Encourage yourself. 25

    Stock up! 26

    Believe what He says. 28

    God has a plan. 30

    God fights for His children. 32

    God cannot be judged. 34

    A touch is all it takes. 35

    Rejoice in the Lord always! In everything give thanks! 36

V. It is well with my soul 39

Foreword

Life is a dance like no other. It cannot be rehearsed, everyone's steps are different, and it just happens, mostly without warning. What may seem to be a perfectly normal day can change its shape in an instant.

We had a plan mapped out, and things were going well. We were doing just fine till Colon Cancer showed its hideous face and robbed us of our normal day. Yet, it is wonderful that we are called to rejoice in this day because it is the day the Lord made. Right here where we find ourselves, in and out of season, no matter the situation, right now, it is the day that He has made.

This is a testimony of God's presence and love at the worst moment of my life: the death of Dalmas, a man whom I dearly loved and grew up with. Anyone who has lost a loved one or who has experienced loss of whatever kind or whose dreams seem to be abruptly growing wings and flying out the window knows the feeling of helplessness and despair that comes rushing in.

At a certain point in life, one's faith will be tested. When that moment comes, I pray that you will have the grace to hold on and to stay in the boat with Jesus. I pray that mercy comes to meet you and that it stays. Life can be a complex, chaotic and an incomprehensible jig-saw puzzle. We do not have all the pieces. Sometimes it hits us with a ton of ashes and we do not know how to move from that place. But God sees it all; He knows where each piece fits. Only when each one is moved to its rightful place will there be meaning. That is the art of the Maker of the universe. He makes everything work for our good; He does not pick and choose, He takes the pricks and thorns, the dancing shoes and flower petals, cries and merriment, and makes them all work for us.

For broken hearts wondering if God can hear you, for weary souls tired after a series of battles, for shed and unshed tears, for seekers of God's voice in this noisy world, I give you my testimony. As I speak to you, I speak also to myself. You will never walk alone; He is watching over you.

The God who stirs up the sea and makes its waves roar, He who stores the snow and calls each star by name, the One who stretched out the heavens and soothes mountains to sleep, will send showers and cause something beautiful to blossom out of the ruins of your life. This book is about God's love. It has to mean something; otherwise these are just random words wasting time on paper.

In loving memory of Dalmas

I lift my eyes up to heaven
And hope you hear my heart calling
Then I close them and see you brighten
And hope you say, "Your hand I'm holding,"
I let God's river sweep my burden
And hope He lets me see you smiling

Introduction

The first time I saw him, I was seventeen and he was standing behind a bush; this, he did not remember. He was fifteen and simply my friend's younger brother who had a Gilbert rugby ball in his hands every other afternoon. My friend's family had moved house making us neighbours. As a result, Dalmas and I became acquainted with each other and in the course of time, we became friends.

Since my dream of working in the medical field had flown out the window, it was time to execute Plan B: French. I had studied it in High School with such great pleasure, so I was massively thrilled when I got my Visa to study in France! Travelling overseas made me lose some of my friends. After a while, communication withered and the wall of silence grew higher, but Dalmas and I kept constant track of each other. "Out of sight, out of mind" to us, was a lie.

We wrote to each other at least twice a month, then thrice, then weekly, and after three years, it was on a daily basis. He was consistent. Trust, the foundation of true friendship, was steady between us.

At twenty-four, God answered one of my major prayers when I least expected it; He brought into my life the exact kind of man that I had prayed for: a man who had reverence for Him, a man with a gentle, beautiful, and caring spirit, a man who was reliable and with whom I could pray. When he boldly asked me to be his girlfriend, I knew "yes" to be the right answer. The intensity of my love for him made me wonder how much more I was to love God. The way He loved me humbled me. If he loved me that much even in my weakness, how much more does God love me? A kind of peace that I cannot fully describe reigned between us.

In our human nature, our connection was special; we had a sixth sense in common. Somehow, despite the geographical distance, we would feel it, deep within ourselves, if something was not right with the other person. Our families and friends were happy for us

1

when we told them that we were together! They were amazed at how well we were doing in our long-distance relationship. We were very present in each other's lives because we wanted to be; we enjoyed each other's company and we laughed a lot. I felt Dalmas' affection in his words and saw it in his actions, I breathed it in his kindness and touched it in his patience, but it was more than that; to me, his love was a glimpse of heaven. At first, I was really scared because I did not think such love was humanly possible. But he was unwavering, so with time, I learnt to accept his love and to love him back fearlessly. Our heart connection grew stronger day by day. We believed that what we shared had God as the author and no one else; it was a miracle for both of us. The search was over; we had found "the one".

We had a "Five Year Plan" in which he was to find a job as an Aeronautical Engineer, what he had studied to become, I was to finish my studies, graduate and go back to teach French in Kenya, and then we would get married and have cake!

Whilst some people were persuaded that I would not make it in my French Literature course as I am not a native French speaker, Dalmas was among those that cheered me on. He showed his support in different ways. He started learning French all by himself. He would find the English versions of the French Literature books I was reading and then talk to me about them.

Without hurting my feelings, he plainly told me when I was wrong. Second from God, I went running to him to fill him in on my day. He did not think I was weird when he found out I love the smell of old books. I thought he was brilliantly weird for excelling in both High School and University without taking notes in every class.

Together, we had painted seven colourful months when our biggest challenge hit us. The Saturday evening that he mentioned Cancer, my stomach sank and I sank with it. "This cannot be happening," I repeated to myself. He had had severe abdominal pains which had been misdiagnosed earlier. He was first given medication for Malaria. Days later, it was decided that he had Typhoid. However, the symptoms persisted and he was taken to a private hospital where proper tests were done and stage 3 Colon Cancer uncovered.

He was broken, I saw it in his face; his eyes had lost their shine. We were broken. My eyes were pregnant with tears, the world was dull and blurry through them. We looked at each other in silence for a while, we both had shattered hearts but naturally, I said, "It will be okay, God has got you." He smiled. We said goodnight and turned off Skype.

The next instants were bitter, red rage rose within me. I was angry with God! Why Lord, what have I done for you to treat me like this? Is this fair? You know we love each other! You know we want to spend the rest of our lives together! So why are you doing this? Why did you bring us together if it was to separate us in the end? Having emptied the fury contents of my heart, I calmed down, and apologized to God for my outrage. I knew that I had nowhere else to go. Yet deep within, I supposed that He was punishing me for something I had said or done.

The next day, I did not want to leave the house; I wanted to stay in-doors and soak in my tears, but I went to church, and thank God I did. I served in the team that welcomes new people to church. My team leader and the rest of the members joined hands and prayed for Dalmas and me. The part of prayer that changed my attitude was, "Lord, help her understand that You are not punishing her, that this could be purely between You and Dalmas for the glory of Your name." At those words, the peace that surpasses all human understanding instantaneously filled my heart. With a new hope, I spoke with Dalmas after church, reassuring him that God is in control. I was even able to study that evening.

It is such a helpless feeling knowing that someone you love is in immense pain but there isn't anything you can do to save them. It was at that time that I truly comprehended that I am not in control, that even though I have a certain amount of power over myself, I am not the master of my life but God is. It is to Him that I lifted my eyes. He sees it before it happens, He equips His children for what He allows to come their way and brings them through. Family and friends from different parts of the world were praying for Dalmas day and night. It felt so good to know that someone was earnestly talking to God about him. This made us hopeful.

He started the first session of Chemotherapy with great enthusiasm. He had a fighting spirit; he wanted to get better. We were honest with each other even at that time; we always let each other know what we were going through. He would message me when he was in pain and I would pray for him, "Lord, he is Your son; You understand what he is going through. You are his Father, so I trust You to take care of him. Heal him Lord, relieve him of the pain. Nothing is impossible with You. We look to You, in Jesus' name." It was hard to concentrate in class; I failed the examinations I was taking at that time. My brain seemed not to function at all. I told him about it and what he said still plays in my head, "To me you are the best, do not worry about what others say. Now go back to studying!" Before he went in for surgeries, we would always read the Bible and pray together through the telephone or on Skype. We were fighting Cancer together. We were not giving up! We had faith, we had hope and we had love. Our love for each other doubled.

Dalmas had told me that according to the doctor, he had about a month to live, but I am thankful that God kept him alive longer. We had not seen each other face-to-face

3

for four consecutive years, so we were massively excited when my flight was booked and the ticket printed! My luggage was ready weeks before my flight! The eagerness was so concentrated within me, I felt like giving everyone a Christmas hug that late July! Walking out of the plane felt like riding on a cloud, I could not feel by feet! Waiting for my luggage was like waiting for an egg to hatch, it felt like years! Feeling my heart dance to a beat within me, faster by the minute, wheeling my baggage outside and then, God bless this moment: seeing him right before my eyes! Seeing him waiting for me with a smile! Seeing him standing on his feet and with no IV on his arms! Nothing else mattered, I was home!

God gave us time to simply enjoy each other's company playing scrabble, laughing to tears, getting caught in the rain, going for walks and praying together. He had told me, before my journey, to write a list of what I would like us to do. I made it plain on paper and one by one, I ticked when an activity was done.

My five-week holiday had flown at the speed of light, marking time for me to go back to Paris. We never said good-bye in our relationship, we never wanted to, not even after a telephone conversation. We would say, "Catch you later," or "Hear you soon," so unsurprisingly, we did not say good-bye at the airport. He held me in his arms and sang to me as I cried on his left shoulder. That was the last time we saw each other face to face.

On a Saturday night, six weeks later, the telephone call that turned my life inside-out came, "Lynda, Dalmas has left us." It took a while before the message sank in. "Dalmas has left us," a simple sentence with one subject, one complement and one verb, why couldn't my mind process it? Dalmas has left us. I sat on my bed with those words flashing in my head. Dalmas has left us! It was a terrible echo; it was dreadful! I was shaking like a leaf! I felt like I was losing my mind! I felt like I had no mind to lose! It felt like a bad dream, a horrible dream! Wake me up! I needed to wake up! I demanded to be woken up! I desperately begged God to wake me up. I waited to snap out of the nightmare and talk with him again. A cry that had been gathering at the bottom of my heart filled my mouth, shook it violently and exploded as if to compete with the explosion of tears on my cheeks. The streams of tears running down my face were as sharp as a blade. My heart was worse than broken, it was ground to ashes. A part of me died that night.

There was no feeling of hunger or thirst, I drastically lost weight. Nothing seemed real to me, nothing made sense. I was a stranger to myself. I felt like a robot. The world was absurd. I felt empty, lost and abandoned. I had lost my home; with Dalmas gone, I was homeless. I could not read the Bible. Every time I made an attempt to open it and look at the words, it felt like my heart was breaking all over again and I would break down. What prayer could I say at that time? Words were hard to find. "Even though You slay me, still I will trust in You," was the sentence I heard myself articulate.

My trip to Kenya this time was not the same. Flipping through my journal in the plane, I read what I had put down the day he asked me to be his girlfriend and said, "I'm in this for the long run." The day he graduated, how happy he was and how proud of him I felt. The day my sister, taking a picture of us at my nephew's birthday, said to us, "Stop pretending he is your son! Get your own!" How we both laughed at her remark. These pictures played and replayed in my head. He had a funny way of saying things. I laughed upon the remembrance of some events and cried upon the remembrance of others. Wondering how it felt, I pictured him walking on the white clouds outside.

As I waited to be picked at the airport that night, I could not help searching for his face in the crowd. He was not there. I looked again, more keenly, but His smile was not on his face and his face was not in the crowd that waited. It was strange that he was not there; it was odd that he would not be there ever again. How do I live? How do I get past this?

When I saw the coffin and then his body, I feebly sat down crying. Lord, do You want to know where it hurts? Well, this is it! This is my desert, my place of brokenness and thirst. This is my fiery furnace, my Red sea. This is where I am one, just one of the five thousand people looking to be fed and there are only five loaves and two fish. This is where doors have been shut in my face. I feel like Moses when You showed him the promised land from a distance, only to tell him that he would not get to it. Still, listen Lord, with all that is in my heart, I sing Kari Jobe's song to You, "Even when it hurts, even when it's hard, even when it all just falls apart, I will run to You 'cause I know that You are lover of my soul, healer of my scars. You steady my heart."

As I looked at his lifeless body, the difference between the body and the spirit became clearer. What was before my eyes was just a shell. His absence in it meant that he was present someplace else: a place where Cancer is not allowed. I had peace about that.

Once I got back to Paris, the most difficult part started. A friend had told me that it would be tough, but I had underestimated the weight that was on me. Stepping back into my normal activities, I went to serve in church that Sunday. If you are to greet people and welcome them, you will need an honest smile, not just parting your lips to display a number of teeth. It was not the same. I made my lips curve to look like a smile but I was torn and screaming inside. I insisted on volunteering the next two Sundays but it was still not as it used to be. I was hearing, not listening, looking, not seeing. It was clear that everything about me had changed and that I had to accept that. This is when I took a break; human strength can only go so far.

On a different Sunday in church, I stood still like an empty tin. As if facing an open sea, I looked on as the rest of the congregation worshipped God with arms lifted high. Their voices rose in praise while I was stiff inside and out. It was the day I was going to give up on God. I had trusted Him since I was nine, when I accepted Him into my life. I had learnt Bible verses by heart. While praying, I had quoted, "By His stripes we are healed, You are Jehovah Rapha, the Lord who heals," yet He did not heal the man with whom I wanted to spend the rest of my life.

My heart felt numb; I wondered whether I had a heart at all. It was a feeling of emptiness and brokenness that wrapped me, a sentiment of loss and defeat. The greyest of grey clouds surrounded me as I chocked in the ashes of my life. I told myself, this is where it ends; while it works for some people, faith in God has not worked for me. It was not out of bitterness that I was leaving, it was out of the feeling of abandonment and defeat. Since I had made up my mind, I could have gathered my belongings and left right then. Why I did not do it I can explain: when I could not hold on to God, He held on to me.

I sat down to listen to the word. One man's testimony made me take courage again. He had gone through a series of tribulations, but the last of them caused an overflow. At that place of misery, fear, aching, and loneliness, walking outside, alone on a cold winter night, he cried out to God, "If this is what I have to go through because I chose You, then I will trust You even more!" Even though my pain did not leave when I heard his story, I got transformed. When he asked those who were going through hurtful situations to stand and be prayed for, I was up before he finished his sentence. Who was looking was of no importance, I just wanted Jesus. During the prayer, I felt a change inside. It was as if I had just been reborn! I had been renewed!

The new creature had to learn to do everything all over again: to crawl, to stand, to fall, to walk, to stumble, to trust, to smile and to attempt to spread its wings. A thirst for more of God came over me and settled in my heart. In the privacy of my room, I sought Him through prayer and through reading His word.

He taught me that what I needed was to step back from the crowd and be alone with Him. In this private place where I found Him, I let Him have my ashes and ruins. It was a session of therapy, a time to learn and a season of growth. He placed a desire in my heart to write what I felt within me. A still, small voice spoke, and I began to write in a journal named "There, Where Everything Changes".

"He shall be called Emmanuel" - Isaiah 7:14

You can talk to me about it all over again. These hands that stretched out for you are well capable of holding you and calming your troubled heart. I know, I understand, I was there. When that call came in, I knew it would. But I also know you; I made you in my image. Do you believe? Do you still believe?

You did not travel alone, lonely though you felt. You did not see me, but I saw you for I am in you, you are in me. Clouds hide blue skies just like the thick, choking smoke of pain blocks your vision of me. But I have seen it all; no single detail concerning you has escaped my ever so sharp eye. Nothing can stop me from loving you, nothing can hold me back. You were not looking forward to this, this is not what you hoped or prayed for, I do understand child. Yes, your heart is fading and your dreams are shaken. I hear what you cannot express.

I see that fear, I can touch that pain. As you walk towards the exit, you are in my arms. You did not ask me to hold you; a good father knows his child's needs beforehand. I am your Father. As you lean against the wall, looking for his face in the crowd, longing and waiting, I am standing right beside you, holding you so you do not fall. My children are my business. I take care of them whether they feel it or not. You are my child. You are my business.

The good, loving and tender memories are being threatened by the valley of the shadow of death. Fear no evil child, I am with you. My Spirit is within you. Emmanuel, remember? I will give you purpose, just wait on me and see. You lay your head down, all is cold and stiff and frozen inside. You ask if time has stopped. You feel like a stranger, which indeed you are. I am your Home; you are walking to be with me face to face. You are just a foreigner passing through earth. When you enjoy the travel, I delight in your happiness, but let the twilight remind you not to get too familiar; Home awaits your return.

I walked where you walk, I am still with you. Patience child, I am bringing you through. Take my hand. We have more to get past. Take my hand. You need it, really you do. Take my hand. Count on me. On the road, in the dark night beyond the horizon, are flashes of lightening. Do take my hand child as I will not stop the tears, not just yet. You need to be free, let it out because I have a jar. Not a tear is forgotten. Not one drop goes unnoticed, not by me.

My words to you right now seem vague. You do know me though, I am resilient. I am not giving up on you. I will be with you for ages. Even when you stood in that dry, darkly, dangerous spot on your way to the coldness of what you did not hope for, even then, I was holding you. Holding you in these hands that were nailed for you.

I see the brokenness and the stiffness of your heart. I feel what you feel; I hurt when you hurt. My love, unlike shifting shadows, is constant. Trust me again; let me be your anchor. These waves are too strong for you. But they hear my voice and they obey.

Put your hand in mine. It is not over yet.

My heart rejoiced when you sang child! When you got to the point where doors closed, hope shook and time stopped, still you sang! Like a hen tucks her chicks under her wings, I tucked you under mine. Do rest in me, take peace and sound sleep. They are yours to keep. Home is with me child.

I gave you those dreams; I put them in your heart. You are not to mourn as though you have no hope. Beside the opened earth you stand, you see the dreaded tree, cut and shaped for the one you loved. They cut and shaped one for my Son too, up on a hill. "The Place of the Skull" they called it. So tell on every hurt and shame and regret. Come with confidence for the table is set.

You will cry and feel overwhelmed, but in my care really you will be. I wrote you a love song before you came to being. I have not stopped since. In every sunset and dawn, in every raindrop and sunray, on every mountain and shore, down the valley and in the darkest cave, in still waters and rushing waves, a love song waits for you. When your world gets earsplitting, indeed it does, step back, hide in me and listen.

Nothing seems to make sense anymore; nothing seems significant either, write it all down. It is all too difficult and surreal but you will wake. Snow and rain hear me and fall, and so will my word. Grass will grow. You will wake, and when you do, my presence will fill you with joy. Love never dies. Love is with you. Love is in you. I am Love.

Angel Girl

After the burial, the crowd gradually retreats. The grieving family walks into a period of intense mourning. The absence of the loved one is deeply felt at this moment. There are no more messages from him, no more telephone calls. When the table is set, it is one plate less. His laundry no longer hangs on the line. The walls testify of the absence of his voice. The house takes a queer, cold profile. As strange as it is, we expect him to walk in at the time he usually turned the doorknob. Silence echoes from room to room causing headaches and tears. His clothes are put away.

We look at his shoes, his favourite chair. We see the fresh grave and his picture on the wall. This cannot be happening, is it true?

Fear gets so real one can hear it breathing. The darkest, deepest horror grips us and we just cannot move. We question our plans, what good are they if life can end as swiftly as a grasshopper's hop? Sometimes we do not even want to go out, and when we do, we find that the world is still going about its business as if nothing happened. Our clocks seem to have stopped whilst that of the world ticks away. How can the world still go on? Does it not realise that we lost our loved one? Does it not see that images of the coffin are still in our minds? Does it not understand that we are hurting? World, can't you stop?

Tears welled up at the sight of her. Dalmas and I would have had a little girl just like her, I thought to myself as they danced in my eyes and slid down my face. I looked away. Turning my head slowly to the right, I looked at her again. She was so peaceful, so calm and with the prettiest face. I loved her, just like that.

The next day, as I was lying on the sofa with a heavy heart and swollen eyelids from crying, I observed that she was looking at me through the window. I started playing an eye contact game with her. I would stare at her for a while, then all of a sudden cover my eyes with my hands. From her laughter, I believed she liked the game.

Quietly, she came and sat beside me. The little shy girl, it came to my attention, was not so shy after all. "Cut my nails," she said and then burst out laughing. This metamorphosis surprised me in a good way. She brought a nail cutter, I sat up and started cutting her nails. Still laughing, she uttered the exact words that Dalmas had said when I last cut his nails: "What? Are you cutting the skin as well?" I felt my lips stretch and I smiled honestly for the first time.

She threw her head back laughing heartily and added, "My nails are so tough; they can break the nail cutter!" More of Dalmas' precise words! At this point, I laughed out loud too and gave her a big hug. She then urged me to have some tea having asked if I had taken some that morning as she had not seen me do it, "Where do you hide?" she asked.

When the nail cutting session was over, she held my hand, led me outside and asked me to sing. I told her that I could not. She insisted, and I mumbled some words of a song I cannot even remember as it was not coming from my heart. When I had finished pretending to sing, she broke into a song that said that Jesus died, but that on the third day He rose again. A part of that song asked where I was looking and said that I should look to Jesus. That is truly profound, I will look to Jesus and not focus on what is happening around me, I thought.

Looking at me with a smile and twinkling eyes, she said, "I have got another song," then she sang Willy Paul's and Gloria Muliro's song, *"Oh sitolia mimi, nafahamu Ukonami […] mpenzi usilie"*. (I won't cry because I know You are with me […] do not cry love.) My mouth dropped open! The song she was singing is the song Dalmas had sung to me whilst holding me in his arms right before my flight to Paris – the very last song I heard him sing! It was incredible! For a minute, I stood there torn between laughter and astonishment! Then the warmest of warm feelings filled by heart as though to reassure me that Dalmas was indeed alive somewhere even though I could not see him. That moment was finding an oasis in a dry and thirsty land.

She followed me around since that day. Leading me by the hand, she sent me to bed at 9pm, saying that she would check on me in the morning. Sure enough, she did! I was pleased to see her, yet she looked at me and asked, "Why are you sad?" I told her it was because my friend had died. She took off her jacket and started fanning me with it saying that my chest was hot. I quietly told her that there was pain right there, (in my heart) to which she said, "That pain will still be there tomorrow."

We got practically inseparable, till time came when I had to say good-bye. She was sad, and so was I.

When we hurt, He puts the right people around us who will be strong for us. There was pain, but there was comfort. She was about seven at that time. Her name is Cynthia, but I call her "Angel Girl".

His voice in the storm

God changed my assumption; my distress is not a scolding but a school. Here is what I am learning:

GOD IS FAITHFUL.

It is heart breaking when you pray and quote scripture yet no positive results arise. Still, God remains true and loyal to His word. He remains steadfast.

In one way or another, God will make you understand what you need to understand. When life happens and we cannot explain, I pray that we will be able to say, "Lord, I have no idea why this is happening, but I trust that You have all the answers and that if it is Your will, You will reveal them to me. If not, then help me to trust You anyway and to have faith that You are with me, that You have a plan and that You will make everything work because You love me."

His ways are above our ways, His thoughts are not like ours, He says so in Isaiah 55. He promises, nonetheless, that His word will not return to Him without accomplishing the purpose it was sent for. It is thanks to His grace and mercy that I still believe He is Jehovah Rapha, the Lord who heals. However, if healing does not manifest itself in the way we hoped it would, then His right hand upholds; He comes through in other ways. He gives us exactly what we need to go through the trial. We were taught to pray, "Thy will be done." –Matthew 6:10.

Endlessly, I asked myself, "Did I not pray enough? The faith I had that God heals, was it not enough? What did I not do right?" These questions got answered one Sunday morning: "God hears prayers. He is not waiting for you to get dramatic in order to give an answer. He is not up there asking you to get louder so that He can move in your situation." He already knows what you need before you ask, Matthew 6:7-8. Even when we do not grasp what is taking place, He wants us to have faith in Him, to believe that He loves us and that He will bring us through.

"It seems clear that we cannot always measure faith by results. Faith is a virtue and value on its own merit. Our faith is not based on what we get; it is based on who we trust." –UCB Word For Today (an international Christian media group, henceforth referred to as "UCB Word")

God is a loving Father. God is a patient Father. God is a caring Father. Nothing kept Him away, not my anger, not my blaming Him, not my asking why. He listened and He soothed me with His word, with His presence and with His gentle voice. He held me, even when I did not feel His presence. He never cast me away. He never sends away those who go to Him.

Nothing can separate us from the love of God. Nothing can stop Him from loving us. Circumstances have a way of blurring our spiritual vision of His love, but when we choose to look to Him, He teaches us to see through the lens of faith. God's love is perfect. It is not based on what we do or what we say; it is based on what was done at the cross and what He says. He conquers by love. The only thing we are to do is accept His love. It is a gift, not a repayment for the good works we have done. When a gift is held out to you by someone who loves you, you say, "Thank you," and you receive it.

EVERLASTING FATHER

Each dry, dead end at His touch blossoms to a new robust beginning
Very hands with patient love line up the stars keep count of the sand
Ever present are they, these hands, to pick up, to rock, to touch
Redeeming, reviving, resurrecting, restoring in time all these
Little bits and pieces of a shattered, scattered, weary heart
Are flown to His hands, these bits, slowly breathed on.
Sores underneath cannot escape His watchful eyes
They search down to the depths of the hidden
Informing, instructing, intervening, inhabiting
Nourishing the new neatly bound heart
Graced with His love Everlasting

Flows within Him love like no other
Anointed, this life extols only Him
The One, True, Strong Tower where
Held captive freely I stand. Secure
Even as repellent waves roll and hit
Rest is mine to find in my Father

TAKE TIME TO GRIEVE

When His friend Lazarus died, it is written that Jesus wept. The Son of the Almighty God broke down and cried, yet He had power to call the dead to life. He did not say to the mourners, "Enough with the crying already! Dry your tears and see the miracle!" No! He took time to mourn. He underlined that it is alright to express sorrow. He is our example.

If there is a time for everything under heaven, as written in Ecclesiastes 3:1-8, then it is important to comprehend the season you are in and to embrace it instead of fighting or denying it.

Crying is a healthy way to deal with the pain, it relieves. Mourning is different from one person to the other. Some mourn longer than others. It is a process that should not be timed or rushed. One is to accept this season, embrace it, and take time to go through it. Those who believe are reminded to mourn with hope: "Brothers and sisters, we do not want you to be uninformed about those who sleep in death, so that you do not grieve like the rest of mankind, who have no hope. For we believe that Jesus died and rose again, and so we believe that God will bring with Jesus those who have fallen asleep in him. According to the Lord's word, we tell you that we who are still alive, who are left until the coming of the Lord, will certainly not precede those who have fallen asleep. For the Lord himself will come down from heaven, with a loud command, with the voice of the archangel and with the trumpet call of God, and the dead in Christ will rise first. After that, we who are still alive and are left will be caught up together with them in the clouds to meet the Lord in the air. And so we will be with the Lord forever. Therefore encourage one another with these words." –1 Thessalonians 4:13-18 (NIV)

I wept that Dalmas went through extreme physical and emotional pain. I wailed for the dreams he had. When his toolbox was delivered to him in the hospital where he was admitted, we were talking on Skype. I saw how eager he was as he opened it, how his face lit up as he checked every piece inside, how his hands keenly moved from one tool to the next. He was passionate about his Aeronautical Engineering course. He had graduated a few months earlier and could not wait to go to work. Because he never got to use those tools, freely, I let my tears run. I cried for the wedding we would never have, and for our Dalmas Jr who would never exist. I moaned for I would never make him a birthday cake, pack his lunch, sit next to him in church again or discuss our children's education. I cry because I miss him.

Some came to me and said, "Do not worry, you are young, someone else will come your way." Does youth shield one from pain? Did these people really think that a chance to love again would be enough to dry my eyes? Weren't they aware and sensitive to the fact that Dalmas was a human being and not an object that could be bought in a shop? I did not find any encouragement in that. Grief does not knock on one's door and say, "I am going to be a part of you for a while. Do not worry though, you are awfully young; you will not feel a thing and your life will not in the least change." We do not simply get over certain things; God gives us the grace to live through them. Some brought up tragic stories for a reason that remains mysterious to me. If they want to, grieving people will talk about what they are going through. But if they do not, just be there patiently. Words like, "If I were you, I do not know what I would have done," could be interpreted as, "I'm glad I get to live my life, yours is miserable!" Grieving people are often very sensitive. Though we may have no ill intentions, our words may sound quite insensitive if we do not pay attention.

We need God's wisdom if we are to encourage someone. He gives generously to those who ask, James 1:5. When moments like these arise and one does not know what to say, a hug is the best comfort that one can give. But if the mouth must speak, then, "I'm praying for you," will always be appreciated.

I WILL RISE AGAIN

Yet I purpose to laugh in the rain
To dance in the dark
To smile on a stony path
And sing even when I see clouds gather
For my pain is known to Him
My tears wiped by Him
My head lifted by Him
Who blows the dark clouds away?
So the blue sky can be mine again?
Who gives me a happy song on the mountain?
A cheer song in the valley
A victory song in deep waters
A calming song in the storm
A cooling song in the fire
With confidence will I leap into the future

Not in my strength, but in His arms
So when another drop comes rolling down
I will lean on His everlasting arms
As I listen to His heartbeat, I will rise again.

THERE IS A WOUND ONLY GOD CAN HEAL.

God has surrounded me with caring friends. I love them, and I know they love me and that they are concerned, that is why they said, "Call me whenever you need me." They were, and they still are very supportive, but there is a wound that only God can heal. He understands what cannot be expressed.

Out of love, we promise to be there for those dear to our hearts. We promise to never leave them, we promise to always lend a helping hand if ever need be, we promise to always appreciate them. But we are limited by our human nature, sometimes we fail.

The one who guaranteed to always be there gets so caught up in life that they forget to call us, or death turns up and we get separated. The one who said would always help apologizes for not being able to, because something of high importance came up. Hurtful statements occasionally come rolling out of the mouths of those we love and we are broken. These people we love, these people we trust, are like us: human! When we look at it that way, we realise that we may have also let them down at some point, and if we have not, we might. Like us, they can only do so much. We get angry, we cry, we ask why, still the best thing is to take it to the Lord in prayer and to remain faithful where God has placed us. There is a reason why we are where we are.

We give our best in the relationships that God has trusted us with, we get disappointed when we are let down, sometimes we become furious, but He helps us to forgive and give a second chance if it is in His will.

We suffer tragedy in this world; it is as simple as that, bad news can show up at any time. Still, in the midst of it all, He gives us perfect peace. Jesus said, "Peace, I leave you with, my peace I give you. I do not give it to you as the world gives. So do not let your hearts be troubled and do not be afraid." –John 14:27

Jesus told the Parable of the Good Samaritan in John 10:25-37. A man was travelling from Jerusalem to Jericho when he was attacked by robbers. They stripped him, beat him and left him half dead. A priest passed by, saw the wounded man, and walked away. A Levite also went over, looked at the man and also walked away. But when a Samaritan saw him, his heart was full of pity. He poured olive oil and wine over his wounds, bandaged them, put him on his own animal, and took him to an inn where he took care of him. He went further and paid the innkeeper, telling him to take care of the wounded man.

But why did the priest and the Levite walk away from the injured man? As a child, I thought that they were purely unmoved and self-centered, but could there be another reason? Could it be that when they looked at the wounds, they feared that they were too complicated for them to handle? Could it be that they did not know what to do? Is it possible that they thought that he was already dead? Is it by chance that the Samaritan had exactly what was needed to start the healing of the man? Who walks around with olive oil and wine for no apparent reason? Is it by accident that he knew exactly what to do? This Samaritan knew precisely where to find an inn, he had no problem paying for it, and the wounds did not frighten him, one may think that this was not the first time he was helping a wounded person.

When walls around us fall and we are deeply cut and all we have are open wounds, Jesus will be our Good Samaritan. When struggles of life attack us, strip us, beat us and leave us half dead, He will revive us through His Spirit and His word. When no one can touch us and make us whole, He will pick us up and have His angels minister to us. He will position the right individuals around us who will help us get up again. When nothing anyone can say or do can bring us healing, He has just the word. The Great Physician knows how to deal with our sores; they do not frighten Him. He will not walk away leaving us alone and wounded. Whilst people may look at our situations and go their way, He lingers near.

He says in Matthew 11:28 (NIV), "Come to me, all you who are weary and burdened and I will give you rest." There is a special kind of rest that only He can give. He calls us to Him so that we can receive it; the perfect peace that makes us sleep soundly in spite of the raging storm. He is our fortress, a place of safety in times of trouble.

This does not mean that we do not need people, we do, but we need to be sensitive to what should be reserved for God. He is the only one who knows what is going on in the hidden depths of our hearts.

Sometimes we just cannot find the right words to say. Other times all we can do is whisper a prayer. Whatever the case, He still hears. If we fall asleep while at it, we can rest assured that He never sleeps or slumbers, Psalms 121:4. There is no better place to doze off than in His arms covered by His presence. So I can say that even though I walk through the valley of the shadow of death I shall fear no evil, for You are with me. So when fear comes in and I feel paralyzed, I know just the Friend to call.

THE HOLY SPIRIT IS GENTLE.

Taking the human form, Jesus experienced what we go through and knew that we need assistance. Before ascending to heaven, He promised His disciples a helper in John 14:16. He describes this helper as one who reveals the truth about God. The Spirit of God is our helper, our comforter and friend. Jesus knew that life can at times be devastating. If He let us have a comforter, He must have known that we would, at some point, be in need of solace. He sent us a friend because He knew that from time to time we feel lonely, even in a crowd, and that we need someone to freely talk to, audibly or inwardly.

Over the years I have been afraid of the Holy Spirit. Keeping my distance, I would say to myself, "I'm good with the Father and the Son, it is the Spirit I'm scared of." The truth is that He has been with me all along because the Holy Trinity is the Three in One. They cannot be separated. When we accept the Son, we accept the Father and the Spirit.

It was during my season of mourning that I first learnt of His presence with me and within me. A new semester was to start soon and the timetable was online. Some of the classes were to take place at the time I usually went to work. This meant that I would only work two days a week and consequently, earn less. I felt so disheartened. I wished I could call Dalmas just to hear him say, "Let's pray about it. God will make things work." I missed him even more. It was difficult to study for an exam scheduled for the next day. Overwhelmed by everything, I sat in bed crying to God that night, unable to find the right words to say. His Spirit came to me in what seemed to be a tangible whisper, and gently, fondly told me to sleep. I did fall asleep immediately. There was no questioning, "Who said that? Why should I sleep? Am I crazy?" Hearing was obeying; I peacefully relaxed into the loving command till the morning light appeared. It was then that I apprehended that He had spoken to me before, with the calmest most peaceful voice, like a down feather walking across my cheek. There was nothing scary about Him; there was only love, warmth, comfort and peace. He is the perfect expression of gentleness. His voice is uniquely sweet, soothing and tender with love. When He speaks, you know it is not your imagination. The next day before the exam, I asked God to show me what to study. I covered most of the work, but for some reason, I kept going over a particular topic. Still revising, a friend came and told me about an interesting class that would start at 8:00am and end at 9:30am! This would allow me to change classes, and work three days a week instead of two! I was so thankful! When the exam came, ninety percent of the questions happened to be on the very topic I could not stop reviewing! That same week, my employers decided I should work late once a week to earn more! I now had four working days! Just enough for a student to live on! I had not prayed for these miracles; I believe the Holy Spirit interceded for me and I am very grateful! He became my resting place and my Friend.

He comfortingly blows whispers of love and peace over my soul. He held me like a thousand warm hugs at the same time. His Therapy is the best. He gave me sound sleep. He counselled me and cuddled me. With every sunrise He gave me new strength. Like Jesus said, the Holy Spirit is with us and within us. Once you personally experience Him, you just want more of Him.

PAIN IS PART OF LIFE ON EARTH.

Does God promise us an easy and safe voyage to heaven? Does He say life on earth will be tranquil? He does not. As long as the sky is above our heads, struggles will come. Jesus said, "In this world you will have many troubles, but be of good courage; I have overcome the world." –John 16:33

Straight lines are drawn by rulers; faith does not guarantee life in a perfect package. In a mixture of spirals, zigzags and moments that seem to be like straight lines in life, faith gives us the wisdom to say, "I know in Whom I have put my hope." Suffering does not always mean we are being disciplined. It is sometimes a reminder that we are not home yet, that we are just passing through earth; therefore, we should not get too relaxed.

God knows what pain feels like. He felt it when His only Son died at the cross for us. Seeing us suffering does not amuse Him. Trumpets are not blown in heaven to celebrate when we face difficulties. He allowed pain to come my way but His love never stopped, it continues, fresh as the morning, as sure as the sunrise. He helps us withstand challenging moments.

We may not know what tomorrow will bring, but without a shadow of a doubt, God will still be loving us; that is the assurance we have. God may allow what we fear the most to come to pass, but He always brings us through because He is greater than all, do not fear.

THIS I PRAY

Teach my soul to rejoice
When the storms of life rage
And my heart to dance
When life plays music that tears me apart

Give my spirit a song
When silence steals my peace
And to my eyes, sight
For what to be grateful for
When all seems lost

Train my ears to hear
Your gentle voice deep within .
When false voices yell defeat
Make my mouth speak
Your words of victory

Do make me mindful,
When challenges stare,
Of who You say I am.
Whenever I doubt, still I pray not to
Let Your love assure me
That You are here
Forever within me.

GOD IS WITH US.

As always, I prayed before going to bed during this time of mourning, yet I experienced a wave of panic attacks. My back would grow ice-cold, sweaty and then numb. I felt as though my heartbeat was in my face. Wondering what was going on, I would shake uncontrollably. My head seemed to swing back and forth in confusion. Reaching for God, I said inwardly, "Lord I know You are here. I believe that You are Emmanuel. Let me feel

Your presence." That silent prayer from my heart reached the heart of God. He opened my eyes, made me sensitive to His presence and I saw that He had covered me with a thick protective blanket. It was dense yet light around me. I was like a baby being rocked to sleep on papa's laps. I felt loved and at peace. I was in the best arms, the arms of Jesus and covered in His blanket of love. Having experienced such closeness with God, when I talk to Him before closing my eyes, I cannot help asking, "Papa, can I sleep in Your arms tonight?"

Each time I closed my eyes, I was certain that I would sleep well because I had prayed. However, a series of nightmares hurried in. I was far from calm. They lasted a week. It was so frustrating. Fear was filling my head and my spirit was so tired, I had no strength to fight. A therapist can give a rational explanation which I cannot rule out, but I went crying to my Father, asking Him to take the nightmares away. That same night though, another nightmare came. I grew totally discouraged. It felt like God was abandoning me. I told myself, if He will not listen to me and answer me, He will surely listen to someone in The 700 Club - a Christian Broadcasting Network program (CBN). Thus I wrote to them, explained what I was going through and asked them to help me pray on this subject.

The first line, when they answered, was, "One of God's names is Emmanuel, meaning God with us. You can talk to Him directly because He hears you." That was the moment things immensely started changing. That was what I had been waiting for all along: the assurance of God's presence.

Sitting back, I spoke to myself again, He is with me, He has always been with me and He will be with me forever! I got so thrilled and the way I prayed changed! I was praying, not to a distant God far up in the clouds, but to the loving God who is on stand-by waiting for me to call on Him, the God that thought of me and sent His Son to my rescue. The God who is in me no matter how I feel! I could approach Him with confidence because He loves me and wants me to be free!

As I talked to Him that night and the nights that followed, He filled me with hope and even gave me laughter! Prayer turned into discussions with Him and so did reading the Bible, "Lord! Did You see that? Jael must have had such courage to drive a tent peg through the enemy's head!" Every now and then, I would be quiet for a while right in the middle of a prayer, meditating on the love of God.

It is a closeness I would have probably never found had I not gone through the hurt and pain that still linger in my heart. As I keep reading His word, His Spirit reveals awesome things about Him to me and fills me with joy even though I mourn.

To fall asleep in a calming atmosphere, I chose some songs that played from the time

I turned off the lights, to the time I rose in the morning. I was afraid, not only of the dark but also of the silence in the night, both of which I appreciated before tragedy hit me. Nine months had passed when I started thinking through this issue, I wanted my life back. I wanted to make peace with darkness and silence. So I talked to Jesus about it one night, got in bed and turned off the lights, with music playing. Right in the middle of the night, my laptop shut down.

Having restarted it, I put the music back on and went back to bed. It shut down again, but this time, I stayed in bed saying a silent prayer till I fell asleep. This happened repeatedly for a few nights. I travelled to Normandy for work some weeks after. There was no need to take the laptop with me as I had put all the songs I listened to in my mobile phone the previous night. When it was time to sleep, there was no music to play as the format I had chosen could not be played by my phone. Even technology can only do so much! With closed eyes, I inwardly spoke to myself, God is with you Lynda, He is watching you, He is protecting you and He is holding you. Do not be afraid. Faith was all I had. Believing that God was with me, I slept peacefully every night for the two weeks that I spent there.

Since then, I have time alone in silence during which I laugh out loud at the remembrance of hilarious occasions, and in darkness when I think about His goodness in my life. Even though I know I cannot go back to exactly how I was before, I am glad that a new me is being modelled in different areas. Jesus defeated the fear that held me captive; He restored me.

Just because we do not see Him does not mean He is absent. He has made Himself available to us no matter where we are and what we have been through. Jesus is Emmanuel and He is true to His name; God is with us. When we seek Him with all our hearts, we will find Him.

I hit the rock bottom and found that Jesus is the Rock of ages. "There is no pit so deep that God isn't deeper still."- Corrie Ten Boom

Darkness, death, disappointment, despair, silence, sickness, sores, sorrow, trauma, tears, terror, life, lack, pain, fear, name it! Nothing can separate us from His love, nothing can keep Him away.

JESUS CONQUERED THE GRAVE!

Before Dalmas took his last breath, death was to me rather distant; it was something that happened to other people. This experience awakened me; the person who had passed away was my soulmate. It made me grasp that life can end unannounced, that all we have is now. No one can tell what will happen in the next two seconds.

A friend asked me, "The Bible says that those who obey their parents will live a long life. Dalmas obeyed his parents, why then was his life short?" For a long time I did not know what to say to that, it saddened my spirit. God opened my eyes, and revealed the answer to me. There are two types of death: the physical death and the spiritual death. Physical death is biological; the heart stops functioning and the body is returned to the soil from which it came. Physical death separates the body and the spirit. Whilst the body remains buried, the spirit either dies the spiritual death in hell or rejoices eternally in heaven.

Jesus died and rose to life on the third day! That is the day that death lost its power; it got transformed into a simple door made of nothing! Physical death is just an entrance into eternity with Jesus for those who believe that He is the Son of God and accept Him.

According to King David in the book of Psalms, God already knew the number of our days before we were born. Can the Lord of Hosts, the Maker of the universe, the First and the Last, the High Judge, the One who never sleeps, be caught by surprise? Is heaven perplexed when someone new walks into eternity having lived the ephemeral earthly life? Does anything happen without God foreseeing it? As we welcome newborn babies with joy, so are believers joyfully welcomed when they are called back Home. This should change our vision of death.

When one is in the darkness of not knowing that death lost and bowed to Jesus, it can be frightful and the situation may be seen as completely hopeless. Light makes us see things for what they surely are. When we have Jesus, the Light of the world, His great glorious glow casts away darkness and displays the accurate face of death: a passage into a face-to-face fellowship with Him.

Jesus said, "I am the resurrection and the life, he who believes in Me will live, even if he dies." –John 11:25

ONE DAY AT A TIME

Sometimes we think too much. As a result, worry and anxiety build within us and end up being too heavy a burden for one day. We worry about things that mostly never happen. This wastes our strength. It is not the will of God. He wants us to take a day at a time. Should one start worrying about the harvest when it is time to plough the land?

Jesus taught us to pray, "Give us *this day* our *daily* bread," not give us this week our weekly bread, not grant us this year our annual bread. Every day is a new day, it has concerns of its own. This revelation taught me to pray differently, "Lord, I pray for strength for this day, I pray for peace for this day, please give me comfort for this day and joy for today." Our Heavenly Father always comes through; He gives us what we need when we need it. It may not come in the package we want it to, but He surely sends an answer.

God has special ways of taking care of us day by day. Each day has its hunger, and each day has its bread. When He provided manna for the children of Israel in the desert, they were to take just what they needed for that day. Those who took too much intending to store some for the next day would wake up to find the pile rotten. Tomorrow's hunger is not to be brought to today's bread. It is a question of trust; He wants us to have confidence that He will see us through regardless of the uncertainty of life.

ALL WE HAVE

Here is today.
Today's sunrise
Today's peace
Today's sunset
Today's trip
Today's strength
Today's rain
Today's wisdom
Today's grace
Today's hunger
Today's bread
Here is today.
Tomorrow
If tomorrow comes
We will call it "Today"

A BROKEN HEART CAN SING.

Sorrow took over my heart, became a part of me and made me different. I lost the desire to sing. Would I ever sing to God as joyfully, as honestly and as spontaneously as I used to before my world fell? Your word says that You dwell in the praises of Your people, but Lord, I am a broken instrument right now, please repair me so that I can give You praise again! At times I called out to God saying, "Please keep me sane."

In Psalms 103:2 (NIV), King David wrote, "Praise the Lord, my soul, and forget not all his benefits." Difficult times can make us forget the goodness of God. They can hinder joy from manifesting itself. They can make us start doubting the existence of God. We are called to praise Him and to remember His goodness right where we are, no matter what we face.

One way joy displays itself is through singing. It does not matter how you sing, it matters what you sing and to whom. The first weeks were difficult. I could not open my mouth to sing. It worried me that I could not force myself to sing. Talking to Jesus about it, I understood that He is patient and that He knows when one's spirit is crushed.

There was no strength in me to make a joyful noise, but I kept listening to my collection of praise and worship songs everyday. One evening, a song tremendously touched my spirit: Michael W. Smith's "Healing rain". I wanted to be caught in that rain! I wanted every drop I could get of that healing rain! I listened to that song every night before going to bed, and each time it was new. From that day hence, a song was sent to my heart day after day. Now and again I would wake up with a song playing in my head, other times it would come to me in the course of the day. These songs gave me peace and reminded me that God cares and loves His people.

"My God reigns" by Darell Evans was the first song that I danced to. This is the time I slowly began to smile from the inside. It opened doors for more songs that I enjoyed dancing to before, and the smile grew wider and greater that I could not contain it! It eventually showed in the physical! From total silence, I went back to my singing and dancing just because I love my God! He restored my soul.

Some challenges are like the thorn that God would not take out of Paul's flesh in 2 Corinthians 12:7-9. The pain did not go away; I learnt to praise through it and to dance for Jesus with my heart in fragments. Praise is powerful; it opens our eyes to God's greatness bringing peace and assurance right in the middle of the storms of life. It reminds us to lift our eyes to Jesus, to call on Him for He is willing and able to rescue us.

A*RISE*

Flap your little broken wings and fly
Find your brittle stolen smile and rise

Feed your fragile smitten heart and sow
Flee those terrible spoken thoughts arise!

Humble heart, gentle spirit
Noble tasks are yours to start
Mumble never, grumble not
Nibble on faith, on hope, on love

When ashes pile and prick your heart
When secret silence reveals your hurt
When the moon is sad and sheds a tear
When stars mourn your sail don't tear

Flap your little broken wings and fly
Find your brittle stolen smile and rise
Feed your fragile smitten heart and sow
Nibble on faith, on hope, on love arise!

ENCOURAGE YOURSELF.

It is wonderful that people can give us timely words when we are disheartened. However, it is important to learn to encourage yourself, to speak to yourself with words of hope, comfort, peace and victory. We can draw directly from God's word and proclaim what it says depending on where we are in the journey of life.

When we are suffering, we are to remember that we are not the only ones in pain, if not, we become selfish and over dependent on the people around us. This could drain them of their strength.

Inspired by David, when I feel low, I speak Psalms 43 to my soul, "Why are you downcast oh my soul? Why so disturbed within me? Put your hope in God for I will yet praise Him my saviour and my God."

When my soul bows down like a chick caught in a storm, I sing Cece Winan's song to it, "Oh my soul, you have not been left alone. For He counted us worthy, so let's be worthy! Just trust and know you're strong enough to carry on. He counted us worthy, so let's be worthy." These words stir it up and make it stand up. Sometimes, when I have a choice to sit down and give up or to stand up and praise, weakness wins. But grace taught me to get on my feet singing, "All to Jesus I surrender." Gradually His peace flows into my soul and my body gets strengthened. Nothing warms a broken heart like a song about God's greatness.

When I get dispirited, Habakkuk 3:17-19 (Good News Bible) reminds me to still look to my God, "Even though the fig trees have no fruit and no grapes grow on the vine, even though the olive crop fails and the fields produce no grain, even though the sheep all die and the cattle stalls are empty, I will still be joyful and glad because the Lord God is my saviour. The Sovereign Lord gives me strength. He makes me sure-footed as a deer and keeps me safe on the mountains."

You need to hear your voice confess positively in matters concerning you. A text message sent by a friend is good but when you draw your strength directly from God, it makes a great difference. You will have something to give.

STOCK UP!

The seven years of prosperity in Egypt were used by Joseph to stock up food for the next seven years of famine. Like we save money in case of emergencies and get medical insurances in case of sickness, we are to be prepared for spiritual storms. Challenges have a way of revealing what we have stored inside. What we choose to believe determines the way we will react in a given position. Theory is put into action when stormy moments come.

Spending time with God in prayer, listening and singing along to songs of praise, reading His word, that is how to get ready. Then when the storm comes, it finds your house built on Jesus, the Rock of Ages, and not a stone will be moved. Those Bible verses learnt by heart and songs will be of great comfort in times of despair. They will strengthen and encourage you.

King David wrote in Psalms 23 (Good News Bible), "The Lord is my shepherd; I have everything I need." While we may not constantly have everything we want, we have everything we need purely because God is watching over us. He sees to it that we get what is essential where we are. David did not write, "I am king, I have everything I need." This is because he had absolute confidence in God's position as the King of Kings and not his own; he surrendered to the care of our Shepherd. He knew and understood that God's magnitude surpasses all earthly crowns and everything they could possibly offer. Even though he was royalty, he humbled himself by calling God his "shepherd". This underlines his full dependence on his creator; the Almighty God who watches over us, He who is always by our side. When we are worn out, He gives us rest, but not just anywhere, in fields of green grass: a place of peace and renewal. He does not leave us thirsty; He leads us to quiet pools of fresh water: a place of tranquility and rebirth.

He gives us new strength when the previous measure has done its duty. He guides us in the right paths. A time comes when we go through deep, dark, traumatizing experiences, like David, I pray that we say, "I will fear no evil, for *You are with me.* Your shepherd's rod and staff protect me." God delights in us; He is pleased and touched by faith no matter how small. He wants our enemies to know that we are His; He sets a table for us right before their eyes and welcomes us as honoured guests. This is because we are precious to Him. He anoints us with the oil of rejoicing and fills our cups to overflowing. It does not matter what life throws our way, He remains faithful and we remain loved. Even in trying circumstances, goodness and mercy will follow us all the days of our lives. His house will be our home forever.

These and other biblical verses assure me of God's presence and support before, during and after the storm. God will not give us more than we can bear. His word helps us endure through it all. Like a footstep is followed by another, somehow one test prepares us for the next.

God says in Isaiah 41:13 (NIV), "For I am the Lord, your God, who takes hold of your right hand and says to you, do not fear; I will help you." When the tempest comes and finds you held in the arms of God, you may cry, you may hurt but you will not be moved. He will hold you and bring you through.

PASSING CLOUDS

If the sun should set
On the dreams You give
Lord cause me to sleep
That I may dream again

If rain should fall
At my party in the sun
Lord may the drops be warm
That I may not freeze in the cold

If I should stumble if I should fall
While running this race

Lord fortify my feet
That I may run till the end

If I should knock at the door
And a friend answers not
Lord hold my hand
That I may not hold a grudge

If I should see a heart
Broken, in the corner in the cold
Lord quicken my step
That I may comfort Your own

BELIEVE WHAT HE SAYS.

Even though he passed away with a smile on his face, I wanted to be sure that Dalmas was alright, that he was at peace, that he was happy in eternity. On the 700 Club website is a section named "Life beyond the grave". It has numerous stories of people who visited heaven and/or hell and then came back to earth. I focused mainly on the accounts of those who visited heaven.

What all these people experienced in common was the love of God. One person said, "You have no idea just how much God loves you. Picture the love of the person who you think loves you the most and multiply it thousands and thousands of times." God really loves us. He truly does. No matter what we do, or what comes about, His love for us is unwavering. There is just no greater love.

Some of them said that they saw their long departed loved ones who were joyful and glad to see them. A man said that he did not want to come back to earth even though he had his wife and children back here. This reminded me of Psalms 84:10, "Better is one day in Your courts than a thousand anywhere." If better is one day with Him, and Dalmas is with Him for eternity, then how happy is he? No sting, no tears, no distress! The grave was conquered, so we are not, and should not be mourning as those with no hope. We will see them again.

Jesus says in John 8:32 (Good News Bible), "You will know the truth, and the truth will set you free." Without Jesus, my situation would say, "Dalmas is gone, lights out, end of story," but with Jesus, it says I will see him again because my Lord conquered the grave. Without faith, my situation says God did not heal Dalmas, He let him down. But with faith, it says God healed him in His own way; there is no sickness, no pain in infinity with Jesus. What is God's word concerning you and what you face?

In His word, God does not reject a tired, and broken heart, He says, "Come unto Me all who are weary and I will give you rest." When fear finds its way into our homes and puts its hands on us, He says, "Fear not, for I am with you. I have redeemed you I have called you by name, you are mine." He goes on and says that He has not given us a spirit of fear but of power, love and sound mind. He promises to be with us till the end of time, therefore we are not alone. He has given His word that if we call to Him, He will answer us, if we seek Him with all our hearts, we will find Him and that if we draw near to Him, He will draw near to us. When life gets too trying and we feel stranded and miserable, His grace will be sufficient.

Knowing what God says regarding us and our situations makes us identify what to accept and what to reject. His word gives us confidence and courage.

In glory

On that beautiful day
Like the sun in May
Tears all blown away
No barrier, no price to pay
I'll hold you in my arms and say
Oh this beautiful day
Like the sun in May

This pain, this fear long gone
Just smiles and peace no groan
Battles of the earth all won
I'll hold you in my arms at home
Pain and fear long gone
Just smiles and peace no groan

Yes I know in Him is hope
I seek His strength to cope
As days go by sometimes I sob
Still I know, in Him, is hope

I will see you again I will
We will talk and sing we will
I am bound to trust His will
Years, just a moment will be.

God has a plan.

In the chaos that we occasionally face, it can be quite tough to believe that there is purpose. We may wonder what good could possibly come out of the issues that bring us heartache and utter confusion.

It takes pages to make a book. Each page is written at a particular time and with a precise reason; it has a role that none of the other pages can play. It takes letters to make a word. When the letter "A" is written, it does not know what letter will come after it, but the writer, the master of the book, knows exactly what he has in mind and how to bring it across.

One cannot read a sentence and assume to master the entire book. Even though there might be continuity from one chapter to the next, new elements will always arise. In the same way, we may not tell what the future holds or see how things will work, but there is a bigger picture. Like a blank piece of paper waits for the author to fill it with coherent words, may we wait on the Lord to give us purpose. He has a vivid project before His eyes, even when nothing seems to make sense to us. "I know the plans I have for you, says the Lord." –Jeremiah 29:11

This does not mean that we are to live our lives aimlessly, waiting for a voice to wake us up in the morning and then tell us what socks to wear and what to have for breakfast. We need to have plans. We are not guaranteed that things will always go as we want them to, we are assured that no matter what happens, God loves us and He will make *everything* work for our good.

It is written that what was meant to harm us will work for our good. God can use the painful experiences in our lives to equip us for what He molded us for, and to help other people. His ways are ever so mysterious. Honestly, I would rather patiently trust Him, than try to understand everything He does or allows to happen in my life. Can man understand the mind of God?

When I felt the burden of pain getting heavier, I occasionally wanted to pretend nothing had happened. But I refused to play strong, I refused to force myself to smile, I told myself that I would grieve for as long as I needed to, I embraced my scar. I wear it like a crown because God has something wonderful at work even though I cannot see it right now.

"He helps us in all our troubles, so that we are able to help others who have all kinds of troubles, using the same help that we ourselves have received from God." –2 Corinthians 1:4 (Good News Bible) What we are going through is not for us to keep to ourselves. Can one say, "He is the Lord that heals," if one has never been sick? Would you believe it if someone said, "God provides," if he has never been in need? When God reveals Himself to us, we need to testify to others. The truth is that behind many smiling faces are broken hearts. It is hard to discern because some hide pain better than others. King David says, "For what You have done I will praise You in the presence of Your faithful people." –Psalms 52:9 (RSV) Tell your story, someone's faith depends on it.

I used to wonder why people say, "Pain will make you stronger." Then I found out that it makes you stronger in faith as you have seen God at work in your situation. Stronger to face another challenge with faith, "He brought me through that, He will bring me through this, nothing is too hard for my God." Stronger to testify of the faithfulness of God in your life; no one can take your testimony away. Stronger in understanding someone going through what you faced; there is a kind of wisdom that comes with agony. Stronger to accept God's way of answering even though it may not be funny. Like I was encouraged by someone else's testimony of God's love, someone's song, and someone's kindness, I hope my story will be helpful to somebody somewhere.

We get disappointed when we have been praying and trusting God to come through in a certain area yet things do not go the way we hoped they would. We feel our hope shrinking. We wonder what we can hold on to because we feel God let us down yet we trusted Him. We wonder if He is really with us. We may study hard, work hard, love hard and give our best yet everything comes crumbling down. There are challenges that seem too big for the measure of faith given to us. That's when His sovereignty comes in, when you have reached your end and the only one you can call on is Jesus.

He did not keep His only son from suffering, even though Jesus had prayed that the cup be taken away from Him, because He had a plan. Notice that Jesus did not force the Father to save Him from crucifixion; He put the Father's will above His own. In the end, He made the name of Jesus glorious over heaven and earth, and sat Him at His right hand, a victorious ending. Unknown, though they may be, His plans are filled with hope, we are victorious in Him.

Be still

We say too late, He says, "Be still"
We say too soon, He says perfect timing
We say now, He says not yet
We say never, He says you think!
We say here, He says patience
We say nowhere, He says here
We say maybe, He says trust Me
We say low, He says rest
We say impossible, He says do you know Me?
We say lonely, He says held
We say defeated, He says strengthened
We say doubt, He says do not!
We say really? He says "I am God."

GOD FIGHTS FOR HIS CHILDREN.

There are times when God saves us yet it takes a while for us to know what we have been saved from. Giving up on my faith would be walking out of the house, away from the protection found under the shadow of His wings. I did not understand it that day, but now I know what I was protected from.

God knew what I would be doing by leaving His boat. He knew that the waters were rough and that I would be stepping outside to be devoured by sharks that were circling around waiting to tear me up.

I would be giving myself away to be preyed upon by the enemy. I would be doing the exact opposite of Rahab's family; they were to stay in the house when their land was being invaded. No one was to get out for if they did, they would not be spared, Joshua 2:18-19. God understood what I did not get that Sunday morning when I wanted to give up on Him. His mercy saved me, He saved the day. He refused to let me walk away broken, unshielded and in despair. He came down to my level and saved me. He fought for me because I am His. He was not going to let me stride away from the safety only He can give. He held on to me when my measure of faith could not bear the agony.

He flew to my rescue; He pulled me out of danger and set me on solid ground. He not only brought me back home, He took me into His arms and held me close to Him, where I am guarded and loved and taken care of.

The road gets dreadful sometimes. We find ourselves facing challenges we have been praying against. The waves of life come crushing against the boats of our lives and naturally, we shake with immense fright. We doubt and want to get out of the boat and jump into the open sea itself, where we only expose ourselves as easy targets. But God is a loving Father to all of us. He reaches out to us and gives us an endless stream of second chances to trust Him again. As long as there is breath within us, we can always go back to Him. He will always fight for us.

PRAYER OF A CHILD

Your Word says to love You with all my might
That I am precious in Your sight
Always open are Your arms
That call me to You just as I am
You will never leave nor forsake me
Till the end of time You are with me
You defend me because I'm Yours
Nothing exceeds this Love of Yours
I have it all, for I have You
All heaven and earth belong to You
Love Everlasting, You put in me
To give it away still, there's lots for me
Never will I run short of supply
For Your Spirit always will satisfy.
You are with me, and in me Emmanuel
With the Three in One, All is well!
I shout for joy for You my Father!
For You hold me like no other
That You, do not cast me away
That You, guide me every day
That I, will be with You forever
Lord You, are truly The Giver

With an open heart I write to say
I love You, and with You I'll stay.

GOD CANNOT BE JUDGED.

At a time when I could not stop asking God why he let Dalmas die, a friend reminded me of the story of Job, whom the Bible qualifies as righteous. He was best placed to judge God. He did not deserve to go through the period of loss that had engulfed him. He had been faithful to God throughout his life. When he was tested, God questioned him in Job 38 (Good News Bible), "Were you there when I made the world? If you know so much, tell me about it. Who decided how large it would be? Who stretched the measuring line over it? Do you know all the answers? What holds up the pillars that support the earth?" Job had no response. He humbly said, "I am unworthy, how can I reply to you? I spoke once but I have no answer (...) I will say no more."

With Job's story in mind, I stopped asking God why He let Dalmas die. I stopped crying saying, "This is not fair." I got to the place where He was all I depended on, the only one I could constantly, timelessly lean on. It startled my heart, even though I have always known that He is great, that thunder obeys Him. It humbled me that He has the keys that open the storehouses of the snow, that He knows who fathers the rain and the drops of dew. I was put back to my place: I am not God, I do not know everything, I am simply His child. He sees what is best and I am to trust Him completely, even when I do not understand the unpredictable nature of life. I stopped throwing tantrums, kept my lips close together, and firmly, obediently held His hand. All I needed to know I knew it then; He is in control. Can man judge God?

In Daniel 3:16-18 (Good News Bible), we read of Shadrack, Meshach and Abednego. Put in the burning furnace for refusing to bow to an idol, they said to Nebuchadnezzar, "If the God whom we serve is able to save us from the blazing furnace and from your power, He will. *But even if He doesn't,* your majesty may be sure that we will not worship your god." These three men recognized the fact that God is able to change situations. They seized that He has the last word. They had no problem surrendering to His will no matter the outcome.

God can erase the trials we face in a blink of an eye, but if He does not, He still remains God. He still remains sovereign. He still remains the maker of the universe. He is not measured by what He does; He is who He is no matter what He does or does not do. He has given us the grace to choose to trust Him even when we don't see a way out. Deciding to trust Him brings us peace and underlines that we comprehend, like Mary Mary sang, that there is nothing too hard for our God; He is greater than all our problems. He can move the mountain or make a way through it, if it is in *His will*. If not, He will equip us for the climb and be with us every step of the way. Whether things go your way or not, He loves you and He wants what is best for you. Do not give up on God. Keep on believing. Trust in the Lord even though you do not understand. Do not despair; choose to rest in His perfect peace.

A TOUCH IS ALL IT TAKES.

God's power is always available to us. At times He brings it to us, and other times we have to go and get it. A friend lovingly brought it to my attention that He is all powerful. She went further, "One of the things they said in church a few weeks back is that despite that, there is a certain amount of that power and control given to us. Strength can be given but only when it is ready to be received."

At that time, I could only testify of God bringing His power to me. Now I get to testify of how I reached for it. The story of the woman with an issue of blood inspired me.

She had suffered for twelve years and had spent all she had on physicians but her condition remained the same. She must have heard about Jesus and how He had raised a widow's son to life. Surely she must have heard that He had healed a Roman Officer's servant with just a word and without the patient in sight. Word must have got to her on how Jesus had healed a man with a paralyzed hand on the Sabbath. She must have thought of how to get to Him. On her drawing board, the crowd must have been her largest obstacle. But she did not get discouraged, she had to be healed. God knows if her plan worked at the first attempt or if she had to try several times to reach for healing.

Crawling passed the crowd while fixing her eyes on Jesus' hem must have been challenging. She must have focused on Jesus not to pay attention to judgmental eyes suggesting she ought to be away from the public due to her illness. She must have been so desperate to have such faith as, "If I could just touch the hem of His garment, I will be made whole." She got to Him, touched it, and the hemorrhage stopped.

UCB Word explains that Jesus would have ignored what had happened and let her walk away, after all she was healed. But He is concerned; He is sensitive, so He asked his disciples who had touched Him. Being God, He knew who had touched Him, but it was about her. She told Him about her suffering and how she had been healed at the touch of the hem of His garment. Jesus was patient and attentive, He listened to her. Only after she had poured out her heart did He say, "My daughter, your faith has made you well. Go in peace." –Luke 8:43-48 (Good News Bible)

Like her, I was at the point where no one but Jesus could make me whole. Nothing else could stop the bleeding of my heart. What I needed was a personal, one-on-one encounter with my heavenly Father. It had to be more than an encouraging email or a text message; it had to be my Papa. I had a thirst for Him. I had to find Him.

Behind my room's closed door, I let myself into His presence in prayer every day. He says to approach the throne of mercy with confidence. I cannot tell whether I was confident or not, all I know is that there was a lot of crying, lying on the floor, kneeling and singing as I showed Him my wounds. There, my wounded soul was being heard and healed.

Every evening when I got home, I could not wait to continue my therapy session with the Wonderful Counselor. I aimed to touch His hem till it grew familiar to my hands. I wanted to leave my fingerprints on it. Never have I been so desperate for God in my life.

Each time, He came down to me and lifted me. It was not obvious to me that I was in His arms because of the curtain of despair that blinded me. However, the more I spent time in private with Him, the clearer my vision became, and the more sensitive I became to His presence.

Personally, touching His hem is a continuous act. With each touch, He is making me whole. Healing can be immediate in some cases, in mine, it is a process, one where God leads me by the hand from where I am to where He wants me to be.

REJOICE IN THE LORD ALWAYS! IN EVERYTHING GIVE THANKS!

It is not easy, when we are in a period of mourning, to put those words to action. In due time, however, God restores. It may take a while, but He will bring back joy into your life.

Gratitude does so much good to us spiritually, emotionally and physically. We read in 1 Thessalonians 5:16-18 that we are to rejoice always and to give thanks in everything for this is the will of God in Christ concerning us.

What should I be grateful for when all I have is anguish?

I thank God for the love that Dalmas and I shared. Is there anything as beautiful as loving and being loved back? We believed in each other and we supported each other. Now and then we differed, but Jesus was the foundation we were building on, He always brought us to grounds of understanding, patience, forgiveness and a multitude of second chances. Praying together, knowing that we were cheering each other on, correcting each other with love, sorting things out instead of running and never being too prideful to apologize. We brought out the best in each other even in our weaknesses. Many are pessimistic about long-distance relationships, but Dalmas and I noted that despite the challenges, if two people who truly love each other willingly work together towards a common goal for the good of the relationship, set their priorities right and devote themselves to the relationship, they will be on the right path. We were always considerate of each other's feelings. Love is beautiful. God's loving character reflects in us for He created us in His likeness. We can only love because He loved us first. Love does not hurt.

I am appreciative of the fact that God gave Dalmas strength to go through the harsh series of Chemotherapy. When we talked in between the cycles, he was weak but His voice was painted with hope that he would get better. He would tell me, "The next session will be in two weeks, I cannot wait to start," and we would pray together. What he went through was hard for those that cared for him, but it was even harder for him. He was so brave. He even kept his sense of humour through it all.

I am thankful that friends rushed in to comfort me, to pray for me, to get me out of bed when all I wanted was to wake up in heaven. God has surely blessed me. My family have been so supportive and extremely patient with me. They never stopped checking on me, praying for me and trusting that I will pull through. Dalmas' family have been of great comfort in many ways. As I pray for them, they pray for me. Even a stranger gave me a shoulder to cry on when I was overwhelmed in a bus once.

When I got back to my University, my classmates were so concerned. I was really touched by their kindness. Some helped me catch up by giving me their notes, others had let the professors know the reason for my absence, while others offered to listen if ever I wanted to talk. I was surrounded by so much love. I had not prayed for the favour I was receiving, sometimes God answers prayers even before we identify the area of need. His Spirit intercedes for us.

My professors were very understanding; some even helped me to study. A time came when I thought to myself, I cannot use grief as an excuse, I need to study by myself! When I got down to it, I would flip through the pages with tears rolling down my cheeks. God always picked me up and gave me strength. Gradually, the ability to concentrate came back. This did not happen overnight. It was a series of trying, falling, failing, being picked up and trying again.

I did not read all the books in the program that semester. Sometimes I could not even get myself to open a book. I would get home and go straight to bed. I am grateful that God qualified me for what I was not qualified for. It is called grace. Remembering my study pattern at that time, I did not deserve to pass my exams, yet He made me victorious all the same. If there is one thing to recall from this: God loves us. He is in control even when things do not happen the way we hoped. He understands that we need Him and He comes through.

I am so thankful for the couple I work for. They showed their support in a way that really touched me. Shortly before Dalmas passed away, I had just paid my tuition fees so my bank account said, "Don't look at me; I will only let you down!" This lovely couple offered me a two-way ticket and I travelled home a day later. Their entire family mentioned my name in prayer: grandparents, parents and children! The littlest at that time innocently came to me and said, "I am going to give Dalmas a call." Her brother remarked, "It is impossible to call dead people." To which she said, "I will call him anyway!" She then picked up her *Dora the Explorer* toy phone, brought it to her ear and began to talk. She came to me minutes later and said, "I have talked to him, he says he is still dead." Her innocence brought a smile to my face.

My landlady, who is also a close friend, was and still is very supportive. When I went crying to her the night I got the call, she said, with tears in her eyes, "I feel for you as if you were my own daughter." She had no encouraging words to give me, but she gave me a handkerchief to wipe my tears and her laps to cry on. True friends are precious.

For family and friends who showed their support through prayer, for those who were there in silence and those who reached out in deeds, thank you. For those songs that uplifted me, held me and comforted me, I am forever grateful.

I give thanks to God for always being available, He is not limited by time, and it is never too late to call on Him. When we talk to Him with openness of heart about how we feel and invite Him into the situation, He comes in and brings a difference starting at the centre of our lives. He becomes our resting place. Every so often, what we think we need is not really what we need. God gives what is best for us where we are. I did not see it that way at the time, but He gave me just what I needed when I needed it. He strategically placed me to listen to a certain testimony, to hear a certain sermon, to read a certain article, to speak with a certain person and listen to a certain song. I am appreciative that He helped me fight the good fight of faith. If it wasn't for His grace and mercy, there is no telling where I would be.

Whatever the season, there is always something to be thankful for.

It is well with my soul

— — —

We live in a world where imperfect things happen. Like the sun shines on everyone, what is happening to *other people* could also happen to us. Believers and non-believers go through the same negative experiences simply because they all live in the same flawed world. The only difference is that believers have said yes to God's offer to help when perplexing situations arise. He makes all things work together for the good of those that love Him.

These unpleasant events in life do not mean that God is non-existent, dead, or insensitive. God is real. He does not stop loving us or being good. Some beautiful things, like fireflies, can only be seen glowing in the dark. Take heart. He does not like it when we lose joy. When our hearts break, He hurts with us. The Bible tells us that God rejoices in us. He wants us to go through life with a joyful spirit. He wants us to invite Him in our journeying so that He can be our anchor when the winds blow wildly. He says in Psalms 50:15 (Good News Bible), "Call to me when trouble comes; I will save you, and you will praise me."

He invites us into His arms just as we are. We are not to say, "I will change certain things about myself first and then I will go to Him." He does the transformation. Our part is to say yes to Him. Jesus stands at the doorsteps of our hearts and knocks, He does not force His way in; He gives us a choice to either keep the door closed or let Him in. If you choose to let Him in, simply say, "Lord Jesus, I believe that You are the son of God. I believe that You died at the cross and rose to life because You love me. I welcome You into my heart today. Guide me in Your ways, amen." Life will serve you mountains and roses, valleys and cool breezes, but Jesus, the Prince of Peace, will steady your heart through it all, you are His child.

Sometimes we feel His presence, other times we feel alone. His promises are not based on what we feel or do not feel. He gave His word that He is always with us. We are not forgotten. Let His voice, His word, His verdict be what you are going to build your life on. He is the firm foundation that can never be shaken. He is for us.

God takes care of His children according to their individual needs and personalities. What is in this book is how He ministered to me. The UCB Word reminded me that Jesus gave sight to the blind in various ways: touching their eyes (Matthew 9:29), spitting on the eyes (Mark 8:23), speaking a word - Bartimaeus' story (Mark 10:52). He even rubbed mud on the eyes (John 9:11). The procedures were different, but the result the same: sight was restored. Go with the prescription God chooses for you. If He puts it in your heart to see a counselor or to join a support group, just trust, obey and take Him with you.

Do not keep what you feel inside. It is too much a burden for you. It will weigh you down and then the people in your world will feel the pressure and may get discouraged too. You are the light of the world, the head and not the tail. Write those feelings down. A healing comes as you empty your heart and as words fill your notebook. A certain power lies in your hands. Talk to a friend who understands, but most importantly, take it to the Lord in prayer.

TAKE IT TO HIM.

Living in purpose where there is no purpose
Living in peace where there is no peace
Living in freedom where everything is confined
God is not intimidated by your problems
He is not shocked by your troubles and sins
He can handle you; He can handle anything you're going through

Holding on to hope when hope seems gone
Holding on to faith when all is lost
Holding on to Christ when it's hard to understand
God does not change like shifting shadows
He is not shaken by your circumstances and fears
He can handle you; He can handle anything you're going through

Getting down to pray when words are low
Getting down to pray when tears still flow
Getting down to pray when it's hard to swallow
God does not despise little faith
He is not looking to criticize and send away
He can handle you; He can handle anything you're going through

A time came when I was wondering what the point of dreaming is if those dreams do not come true. His word came to my heart: without faith, it is impossible to please God. Dreams are to make us dependent on Him. He places some of them in our hearts. As we run after them, we believe that we will get there. That is the point, believing against all odds. Some come true whilst some do not, it is the way there that makes it worth it. Travelling towards them and giving our best sharpen our understanding. They open our eyes to the beauty that can only be seen when we dare to make a dream come true.

My life has changed forever; I accept and embrace that truth. My angle of view has shifted for the best. There are times when I am tempted to complain about what may not be going well, but a gentle voice reminds me that God is still good, and that I should give thanks even though I may not be where I want to be. Inspired by Jesus' prayer before crucifixion, I present my request to God, but I am learning to be open to His way of answering, "Never the less not my will but Yours be done." Focusing on prayer primarily as a sure means of receiving is what I used to do before I learnt, the hard way, that there is more to prayer than that. The "not my will but Yours" part is a constant reminder that indeed God has a plan, and trusting Him means agreeing with Him concerning it even though we may not fathom; the will and intentions of God are not always ours to find out, Ecclesiastes 3:11 (Good News Bible), "He has set the right time for everything. He has given us a desire to know the future, but never gives us the satisfaction of fully understanding what he does." Fully, truly and willingly being in agreement with the concealed will of God is one of the hardest things I've had to do, but it is so liberating once one starts living it. It underlines that we are dependent on God, with brimful confidence that He knows what is best for us.

My relationship with God is on a different level. I know Him not only as the Judge and Eternal King who made heaven and earth, but also as my sweet Papa, my closest friend, my joy, my confidence, my peace, my rest and ever present comforter. I know His voice. I know His warmth. My faith now says that God hears my prayers, and whatever the outcome, He is the Master, He has a reason and He loves me. In this unstable world, He is constant. I choose to look to Him.

The thought of being disconnected from Dalmas does not bring a beam to my soul. There are days I wish I could go back and talk to him. Special days like Christmas, his birthday or mine, may bring tears to my eyes, yet there are days when I feel strong even though I miss him. God makes everything beautiful in its time. How He will make something beautiful out of my wounds and brokenness is not clear right now, but someday it will be. What I know for sure is that He is faithful; I have put my trust in Him. Nothing is too hard for Him; if He allows something to happen in our lives, it is to use it not only for the Glory of His name, but also for the good of others, and for our own good, although we may not see or understand how.

God is greater than everything that has happened, than everything that is happening and anything that could happen. There is no name greater than the victorious and powerful name of Jesus.

For a change, be the one that calls that friend who always checks on you. Be the one to ask, "How are you? How was your day? What can I pray for concerning you?" Be genuinely interested in other people, you have so much to give. Covered by mud or not, gold is still gold. Even in that state, you are somebody's answered prayer, you are someone's blessing, you are somebody's miracle, do not lock away your talents. Use what you have in your hands, start where you are. Like the three servants had to give an account of the talents their master gave them in Matthew 25:14-30, at some point we will give an account of the life God trusts us with; be willing to move forward and bear fruit, with God's help, even though you grieve.

You may get to a place where you ask yourself, "Why am I here?" If you are there, He sees you and there is a purpose. If there is a painting, there is an artist. Is it not extraordinary that you are the only bearer of those fingerprints? You have a unique identity. You were designed to do what only you can do, in a way only you can do it. It may not be spectacular or glamorous; it may be as simple as a drop of water, but remember that small things have immense consequences. Do not despise yourself.

An eagle is not sent to a duck school to learn how to fly. A duck is not sent to an eagle school to practice graceful swimming. So beware of the business of feeling sorry for yourself whilst comparing your situation to that of others. It is not worth it, we are not competing. You have your own measure of faith, and your own life to live. If God lets you walk down a stony path, He will be there with you. In Him, you will have what you need where you will be. You are not alone, you are loved.

In every decision you make, take the name of Jesus with you. You will make mistakes because you are human, but factor faith into everything you do. Keep dreaming and doing your part so those dreams come true. God knows when the time is right, do not give up. Make those petite steps by faith knowing that He is with you. Let these three remain in your life: faith, hope and love. Faith makes us acceptable to God and keeps us walking, hope helps to endure harsh realities of life and love binds everything together in perfect harmony.

If a time comes when you feel it in your spirit to be alone, retreat from the crowd.

Remember, however, that you are a branch that should stay connected to the Vine: the Lord God Almighty who upholds you. Stay in contact with someone who can honestly pray with you. Take time alone with God, talk to Him about everything and anything the same way you talk to the person who loves you the most. God is more into intimacy than formality with us. He is the King of Kings and deserves utmost respect, but He is also our Father and Friend. An open, honest, close relationship is what He desires to have with us. This is found behind closed doors with just the two of you in the room. It is about you speaking to the best Therapist of all time. He knows what you need already, but when you say it, you get to empty the basket before His eyes; You release it from yourself. His burden is easy and His yoke is light.

"We give Him our pain and sorrow and He gives us His joy and peace."-UCB Word

Do not rush this time in privacy with Him; it is there that everything changes. Draw your strength from God first, and then join the crowd again. When Jesus was overwhelmed before crucifixion, He took time alone to pray. He began by distancing Himself from the disciples, taking only Peter, James and John with Him, to whom He said, "Stay here and *keep watch with Me.*" Then He went a little further by Himself to pray, Matthew 26:36-38.

Guard your heart. If you notice a trace of bitterness, regret, unforgiveness, doubt, fear, or anything else that is not in line with what God wants for His children, do not ignore it. Open up your heart, talk to God about it and ask Him to transform you. Forgive those who have wronged you, let God be the one to judge. Let go of the things you cannot change. I pray that He brings back every lost smile and laughter, may He send a flood of songs where there is despair, and shine His light to dispel the darkness of brokenness.

As you pay particular attention to your soul, feeding it with the Gospel of Christ, do not neglect your body. Keep taking care of yourself. You will shine with the rainbow again. With thanks giving, take pleasure in the little gifts that life offers.

Why do I love God? Why do I want to know Him more? For the things He has given me? So He can give me more? For the promises I can claim in His word? For miracles, signs and wonders? To get to heaven? Why do I love God? If I am to love the Lord, then let me do it because He is God and He loved me first, not because of the lovely benefits that come with faith. If I am to tithe, let it be out of thankfulness that He is my source and not just to have the gifts that come with faithful tithing. It is biblical truth that all good things come from Him. I am grateful when blessings are flowing in, His gifts are wonderfully perfect, but I do not want to build on blessings and miracles and gifts. I have to build on Jesus; all other ground is sinking sand.

In Isaiah 61, (Good News Bible) God wants to bind up broken hearts, to comfort those who mourn, to give them a crown of beauty instead of ashes, the oil of joy instead of mourning and a garment of praise instead of a spirit of despair. "They will be like oaks of righteousness, a planting of the Lord for the display of His splendor." Brokenness is a passing cloud. One can cage a bird but one cannot stop it from singing. Joy is never taken away by the circumstances of life; it is a fruit of the Holy Spirit who is eternal. The blue sky will wake with a bluer, brighter face, and the sun will shine again. On that very day, the cage will break open; the darling bird will fly out, she will build a nest, and then, she will sing a new song.

Until then, I am an echo of Job's voice, "The Lord gave and the Lord took away, blessed be His name." With confidence in Emmanuel, I raise my hands and sing, "It is well, it is well, with my soul".

I WILL WAIT ON YOU

Until You divide the water
Until Your cloud moves
Until You send a word
Lord, I will wait on You

Until You move the star
Until You send wise men
Until You show me a manger
Lord, I will wait on You

Until You wake me up
And have me count the stars
Until You pass at night by my row of sacrifice
Lord, I will wait on You

Until You call me down
Until You speak a word
Until You come to mine
Lord, I will wait on You

Until I push past the crowd
Until I get to You
Until I wipe Your feet
With my hair with my tears
Lord, I will wait on You

Until I crawl Until I bow
Until I call Until You turn
Until I touch the hem of Your garment
Until I see You face to face!
Lord, I will wait on You